# DIFFERENTIATION
## Pocketbook

**By Peter Anstee**

Cartoons:
Phil Hailstone

Published by:

**Teachers' Pocketbooks**
Wild's Yard, The Dean,
Alresford, Hampshire SO24 9BQ
Tel: +44 (0)1962 735573
Fax: +44 (0)1962 733637
Email: sales@teacherspocketbooks.co.uk
Website: www.teacherspocketbooks.co.uk

*Teachers' Pocketbooks is an imprint of
Management Pocketbooks Ltd.*

Series editor – Linda Edge.

© Peter Anstee 2011

This edition published 2011.
Reprinted 2012, 2013, 2015, 2017.

ISBN 978 1 906610 31 9

E-book ISBN 978 1 908284 78 5

British Library Cataloguing-in-Publication
Data – A catalogue record for this book is
available from the British Library.

Design, typesetting and graphics by Efex Ltd.
Printed in UK.

# Contents

# Foreword

A glance at the history books or a Dickens novel reminds us how far education has come since the days when students sat silently in rows memorising the knowledge imparted by the teacher; the days when learning was passive and every student received the same provision; when the only differentiation for a child was a consequence of its gender and its family's place in the social hierarchy.

Education has been through a long and liberating transition from a sexist, class-ridden model based on instruction, to one based on teaching, to one based on teaching and learning, and finally to one firmly centred on learning.

Putting learning at the centre means that differentiation is now a fundamental part of a teacher's work. Our focus has rightly shifted from students in general to groups of students and individual students.

# Foreword

Teaching, these days, is an incredibly busy and intense job. It can seem like we're hacking our way through the jungle to get our students to the other side, but seeing them get there – enabling them to learn – is immensely rewarding.

In the modern school where learning is paramount, the role of the teacher, far from becoming incidental, has paradoxically become more complex and important. No longer do we simply manage the knowledge acquisition of silent students; now we are **leaders of learning**.

Stephen Covey describes so well the difference between managers and leaders:

*'Managers are often so busy cutting through the undergrowth that they don't even realise they are in the wrong jungle. A leader is a person who climbs the tallest tree, surveys the entire situation and yells: 'Wrong jungle!' '*

*Stephen Covey: The Seven Habits of Highly Effective People (1989)*

# Foreword

We all need to step back occasionally, not just to check we're in the right jungle, but to consider how effectively we are helping our students through it.

**Be prepared to climb the tallest tree.**
Teachers need to be leaders to maximise the learning of groups and individuals.

To pursue the metaphor, not all students will negotiate the jungle in the same way:

- Some will find it relatively easy; others will lack confidence
- Some will thrive when faced with the challenge; others will need greater support
- Some will think logically about the best route through; others will go charging forward, and some will freeze with uncertainty
- Some will emerge as leaders themselves, etc

It is our job as teachers to lead each of these types of student to success, and differentiation is vital to that process.

# Why
# Differentiate?

# What is differentiation?

How often do we step back and think about what the words we use *really* mean? Not just what they mean in dictionary terms, but what they mean in terms of our values as teachers and how we put those values into action.

The basic question, *'What does X mean?'* in turn triggers many more questions. Let's try it when X stands for differentiation:

- How important is **differentiation** in our provision?
- What are our core principles regarding **differentiation**?
- Which strategies are key to successfully implementing **differentiation**?
- How effective is our current **differentiation** provision?
- How could it be improved?

Whilst this chapter addresses the question of what differentiation is, the remainder of the Pocketbook provides guidance and strategies to help you answer follow-on questions such as those above.

# A definition – or two

The dictionary reveals two relevant definitions of the word *differentiate*:

- To distinguish or show the difference between
- To make different by alteration or modification

The second sense will have more resonance with teachers – differentiation is, in essence: **modifying a lesson or parts of it for one, some or all of the learners.**

The first sense is also pertinent to education. Much as the markings on animals help us to tell them apart, we can differentiate between students on the basis of their prior attainment, learning preferences, target grade, skills, special needs, etc. Modern teachers and schools have a great deal of knowledge about their charges and are highly adept at differentiating *between* students (identifying the differences between them). However, it is so much more significant when we differentiate *for* students (modify classroom provision to accommodate them).

The 'distinguishing' information is useful, but true differentiation should **enable**, not **label**.

# Why does differentiation matter?

Differentiation matters because children and their learning matter. Few teachers would disagree with this; yet (according to inspection reports and academic research) well planned and effective differentiation remains remarkably elusive.

Why might this be?

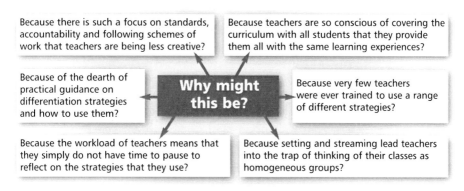

Because there is such a focus on standards, accountability and following schemes of work that teachers are being less creative?

Because teachers are so conscious of covering the curriculum with all students that they provide them all with the same learning experiences?

Because of the dearth of practical guidance on differentiation strategies and how to use them?

**Why might this be?**

Because very few teachers were ever trained to use a range of different strategies?

Because the workload of teachers means that they simply do not have time to pause to reflect on the strategies that they use?

Because setting and streaming lead teachers into the trap of thinking of their classes as homogeneous groups?

# But don't believe everything you read ...

...There are many, many classrooms where differentiation is commonplace.

Enter many primary classrooms to find a highly sophisticated form of organised chaos. Students with a wide range of skills, often from different year groups, are undertaking varied tasks. They work individually, in pairs or in groups; they access help when they need it; once finished they begin the next task.

Enter many secondary classrooms to find exemplary practice where students negotiate individual tasks, where diverse group work strategies involve all learners in ways that suit their aptitudes and needs; where resources are adapted to support and challenge different learners and where assessment informs individual target setting.

These students are not squeezed into a 'one size fits all' mould. They are **active participants** in their learning with the teacher as leader, not instructor.

# The benefits

Smooth-running lessons that accommodate a wide range of individual needs require planning, the kind of creative, student-focused planning that reminds you why you became a teacher in the first place. Just as motivated, inspired students complete work more quickly and to a higher standard, teachers who liberate themselves to plan creatively experience the buzz that only teaching can bring.

The reward lies in focusing on students and their learning, the best ways in which to engage them and get the best from them, ...and then seeing their response. The teacher ceases to be a deliverer of content and behaviour manager and becomes a **facilitator** and **guide** in students' learning.

And with that come:

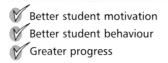
- Better student motivation
- Better student behaviour
- Greater progress

Quality learning

# Each child is different; each learner is different

Learners come to us with different:

- Life experiences
- Language skills
- Talents
- Attitudes
- Learning skills
- Confidence levels

- Prior knowledge
- Commitment
- Ways of learning
- Degrees of home support
- Social skills
- Likes and dislikes

Thus, students have different starting points and different skills in relation to a task and will learn in varied styles and at varied paces.

Differentiation aims to take account of these differences and provide the best way forward for each child.

# Progress

Any judgement of the quality of teaching is based on **individual students** making appropriate progress, ie on **learners learning**.

Providing the same for every student cannot achieve this.

Effective provision must build from the point where each student currently is and help them to move towards where they could be.

Thus, to engage, motivate and get the best from each student, **differentiation is at the core of good teaching.**

# Flow

Psychology professor Mihaly Csikszentmihalyi used the term 'flow' to indicate the state we can reach, in any aspect of life, where we become absorbed in a challenging task and our progress brings personal fulfilment and the motivation to continue to a new challenge and further progress.

In education, this occurs where the **level of challenge** for an individual student is balanced with them possessing the **right skills** and receiving **appropriate support** to meet that challenge successfully. This maximises learning, or creates 'flow', since as Csikszentmihalyi writes:

*When goals are clear, feedback relevant, and challenges and skills are in balance, attention becomes ordered and fully invested.*

Mihaly Csikszentmihalyi: *Finding Flow* (1997)

# Flow – getting the balance right

Excellent differentiated teaching will set tailored challenges for individual students to help them move forward from their existing skill levels. To maximise progress, it is vital that we provide both a high level of challenge and a high level of support. Csikszentmihalyi explains the possible combinations and outcomes thus:

| Level of challenge | Sufficiency of skills and support | Outcome |
| --- | --- | --- |
| Low | Low | Apathy |
| Low | High | Boredom |
| High | Low | Frustration |
| High | High | Flow |

For Csikszentmihalyi, flow is not easy to achieve and requires effort. In his words: *'It takes energy to achieve optimal experiences'*. When we put in the effort and the balance is right, flow leads to personal growth.

# Creating flow

It is only really in the differentiated classroom that it is possible to create **flow** for individual students and groups of students.

- In every classroom, the level of **challenge** that each student can succeed in by stretching themselves will vary immensely
- In every classroom, the **skills** (learning and personal) that each student will bring to that challenge will vary immensely
- In every classroom, the types of **learning** and **support** that students will need to meet that challenge will vary immensely

This blend of challenge, building on existing skills, and appropriate learning and support are at the heart of good practice in differentiation – and at the heart of the strategies and guidance to be found in the rest of this book.

# Creating opportunity

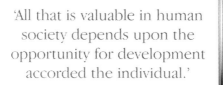

'All that is valuable in human society depends upon the opportunity for development accorded the individual.'

**Albert Einstein**

# Ability, Potential and Difference

# Your starting point

Ask yourself, or ask a colleague who has observed your teaching, how you adapt learning for individuals or groups of students; or better still, *ask your students*.

You will find that you already do more than you think. You might already:

- Vary the types of questions that you ask and who you direct them at
- Group students in different ways for different tasks
- Use Learning Support Assistants and other adults to provide targeted support
- Alter the complexity of your language for students of different ages or aptitudes
- Provide modified worksheets for certain students

# Getting it just right

Too little differentiation treats students as all being the same.

Too much can result in a frenzy of activity with too little focus.

**The right amount of differentiation will maximise learning**

Imagine differentiation as a continuum: at one end is whole class teaching and at the other a fully individualised menu. Aim to find the right place on the continuum for you and your students, one that caters for groups and individuals and that students (and teacher!) can cope with. This position is not fixed – it will shift according to class, task, circumstances, etc. It is likely, though, that as you increase your differentiation repertoire over time, you will edge closer towards individualised provision.

Whole class teaching

Individualised provision

# What is ability?

Traditionally, the way most teachers, schools and advisers begin to plan differentiated learning is to consider students of different 'ability' levels. But what is ability? How secure a foundation do we have if we classify our students as higher, middle or lower ability?

If we attempt this, we are building on shifting sands. There is no generally accepted definition of ability and no generally accepted way to measure it.

Most modern measures of ability are simply a measure of performance in particular assessments. However, many students underachieve in assessments for a multitude of reasons, from attitude to the mode of assessment not suiting them.

Thus, we might wish to view ability in terms of intelligence or skills, but these are vague indicators and even if we could clarify them, how would we measure them?

# What *do* we know about ability?

We know that no-one simply has a certain level of ability. **Ability is complex and variable**; it is sensitive and in a state of constant flux.

Students are more able in some subjects than others. Their ability even varies within subjects: a consummate writer might not be an articulate speaker; a student who has mastered algebra might struggle to grasp trigonometry; a talented footballer might panic at the prospect of having to execute a forward roll.

To what extent we are born with certain aspects of ability or predispositions is unclear, but what is definite is that ability can grow – and it can diminish. With guidance, practice and curiosity, the bizarre patterns on the page merge into words and our ability as readers increases. However, a young child who does no reading during a six-week summer holiday loses some of that ability.

# Ability is too complex to grasp

So, ability is an immensely intricate and fragile blend. Although for the vast majority of students their ability in different things develops as they get older, some aspects grow faster than others, some stagnate for a while and others leap forward as something clicks into place. This growth doesn't just happen with the passage of time; it is the result of learning.

Amongst the students who emerge as high performers in secondary school are many children who were slow starters in education. These will include: summer-born children, children from disadvantaged homes, and boys. Many of them don't really get into their stride educationally until they are into their teens, but with the right mindset and the right teaching they can make tremendous progress.

Good differentiation allows for this complexity. Don't use a narrow definition of ability to classify students: focus on enabling their ability to grow.

# Fixed and growth mindsets

For decades, education was predicated on the idea that we each have a certain level of intelligence or ability that can be measured and that is fixed for life. The work of Carol Dweck and many others has shown that ability can grow.

Through a combination of **effort, motivation, hard work, challenge and support** students can become more able. Students with what Dweck terms a *growth mindset* will believe in this process. They will become increasingly able and will see the value of effort. Their progress will motivate them further.

By contrast, those who have what Dweck terms a *fixed mindset* believe that if they can do something, it is because they are talented in that area; if they cannot do it, it is because they lack talent in that area. They will not value effort and will make less progress.

*Growth mindset* students know that hard work helps them past obstacles in their learning; while *fixed mindset* students are more likely to give up and lose motivation.

*Carol Dweck: Mindset: The New Psychology of Success (2006)*

# How to differentiate *for* ability, not *by* ability

To differentiate *by* ability misses the point – it is too simplistic to categorise students in this way. To deliver quality learning, we have to differentiate *for* ability by:

- Encouraging a growth mindset amongst our students
- Being vigilant for those whose ability emerges late and who can progress rapidly
- Enabling all students to progress to their full potential, ensuring that at times they struggle and have to tackle obstacles
- Ensuring that challenge is always provided and that those who are motivated and ready to do so can access more demanding work

Differentiation *for* ability does not involve different provision for the more able, the middle ability and the less able; it involves provision for *all students* to develop their ability to the next level and beyond.

# Stretch and support

Never let your students rest on their laurels. They should always have a **next step** to move on to, a more challenging question or concept to tackle, a sense that there is more to learn. Whilst getting full marks in an assessment might be a magnificent achievement, full marks in several similar assessments is a signal that a student needs a new challenge – they are *succeeding*, but what are they *learning*?

**Support** is equally vital for all students to ensure that they are being **stretched** appropriately to enable them to make maximum progress. If students always cope without needing support, challenge them more. If they need constant support, consider challenging them in different ways, or a little less.

Few things motivate students better than knowing they are learning and successfully meeting new challenges – take every opportunity to reinforce this.

Stress that whatever level a student is currently performing at, they can stretch themselves and you can support them to improve it.

# Potential, not performance

75 years ago Lev Vygotsky criticised the practice of judging a child's developmental level through independent tests and using this judgement to determine what provision should be made for them. Such judgements are made, Vygotsky states, *retrospectively*, whereas we should judge development *prospectively*. Consequently, provision should be based on what a child *could* learn with guidance; on where they *could* be tomorrow, not where they were yesterday.

A student can achieve more with help and guidance than they can independently. Providing that guidance is why we became teachers. Learning thus becomes a progression:

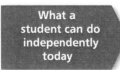

| What a student can do independently today | What a student can achieve with support and assistance | What a student can now do independently which before they could do only with help |

*Lev Vygotsky: Mind in Society (1978)*

# The Zone of Proximal Development

Vygotsky defines the Zone of Proximal Development as the distance between the current performance of a student and *the level of potential development as determined through problem-solving under adult guidance or in collaboration with more capable peers.* Thus, the amount of learning that a student can achieve (the extent of the zone that they can cross) is maximised when you give them tasks that acknowledge their potential and you ensure that they have the support to get there.

Although it is most commonly teachers and support assistants who guide students through this process, it can also be parents or other students. Sometimes, it will be during collaborative group work that others provide help, without necessarily being conscious that they are doing so. Interacting with others and articulating their own ideas are invaluable parts of students' learning. The role of parents – particularly in supporting early progress in literacy and numeracy, but also in answering countless questions and helping their children to surmount obstacles throughout their education – cannot be overestimated.

# Differentiating for learning potential

Great teachers lead their students through their individual zones of proximal or potential development, from where they are now to where they could be. We can do this by ensuring that our lessons are differentiated so that:

- Each student is engaged and motivated by **learning and developing**
- Each student receives **the right level and types of challenge** to ensure that they are progressing as well as possible through their zone
- Each student has **the support that they need** to enable them to meet challenges and achieve their potential

# Ability and learning potential

Putting our focus on potential in this way can radically alter our perception of students. The Zone of Proximal Development, Vygotsky says, allows us to determine 'the child's immediate future and his dynamic developmental state'.

A child's *dynamic developmental state* is the degree of progress that they could make in their learning. Two students might have performed at the same level in their last assessments, but one might have far more **learning potential** on the next task than the other. Students progress at different rates at different times. The learning provided should help them both to fulfil their individual potential.

This points up the danger of differentiating **by** ability – by a measure of past independent performance – and redirects us towards differentiating **for** ability.

> Differentiation seeks to guide each student through their zone of proximal development, to develop their ability by helping them to do independently tomorrow what they need help to do today.

# How else should we approach differentiation?

Whilst differentiation for ability is the most prominent and common way to approach thinking about provision for the different learners in front of us, it is not the only difference that we can or should take note of. Here are just a few others:

- Gender
- Background
- Learning preferences
- Individual interest

The following pages take a brief look at each of these as a focus for planning differentiation.

# Mind the gap

**Girls** tend to be more empathetic, sharing and neat. They are good with people and realise sooner than boys that success requires effort. Their earlier grasp of literacy skills means that they make better progress in the early years.

**Boys** tend to be more active, impulsive and competitive. They are good with systems and want to succeed – only quickly. As their literacy skills develop and they realise that effort matters, the attainment gap narrows.

There is, of course, far more difference within each gender than between the 'average' girl and the 'average' boy. We need, though, to be mindful of the typical differences between the genders to ensure that we differentiate effectively.

# Learning for girls and boys

For both genders to succeed, in education and beyond, we need to **develop their strengths** and **address their weaknesses**. This means providing a range of strategies, some ostensibly girl-friendly and some ostensibly boy-friendly.

At times, encourage all students to share, to put themselves in someone else's shoes and to pause to reflect and take pride in their work. Provide early support for any students whose literacy skills are weak. Thus, girls are encouraged in the areas where they are traditionally strong and boys are supported in developing empathy and literacy and in taking appropriate care with presentation.

At times, encourage all students to take risks, to be competitive and to work at pace so that they cannot be methodical. Value ideas and skills above how they are presented. Thus, boys are encouraged in the areas where they tend to be strong and girls are supported in developing confidence and speed and in getting away from the tendency to equate neatness with quality learning.

# The impact of background

Since ability is developmental and sensitive, it is clear that background can affect the skills a child has developed before they start school. Just as boys can fall behind all too easily, so can children who are in care; who come from disadvantaged homes; whose parents lack literacy skills; who are from minority communities or races; or who are summer born. Not all fall behind, but too many do.

A disproportionate number of these children end up in bottom streams, sets or groups, their background and slow start in education perhaps seeming like a lack of ability. A decade later some catch up, but many underachieve and become disillusioned or disruptive, apparently justifying their place in lower ability groups.

As awareness of these issues has increased, differentiation in some schools has begun earlier than ever to try to reduce the negative impact that background can have. **Intervention at a young age**, particularly in literacy skills, is helping to close the gap between hitherto hindered children and those from backgrounds that have a positive impact on a child's future.

# Learning styles theory

As more attention has been paid to *how* students learn rather than simply *what* they learn, learning styles theory has grown exponentially.

- Bandler and Grinder developed the concept of Visual, Auditory and Kinaesthetic Learners
- Gardner suggested that we do not have one intelligence, but several, which he termed Multiple Intelligences
- Gregorc defined four types of learner according to how we perceive and process information

These are just three from dozens of theories by which we can try to classify learners – there are enough to fill a Pocketbook!

How useful are these theories for teachers seeking to improve their use of differentiation? Remember that in each model, what emerges is a *profile* of learning styles, where some score higher than others. No student has just one learning style and many have no clear preference, so no student should be labelled an *x* learner, a *y* learner or a *z* learner.

# Learning styles and differentiation

Determining learning styles will not produce differentiated learning for the individual.  As well as defining students rather than allowing them to define themselves, it can simply make them more confident and comfortable in that type of learning and less so in others. The danger then is that we create rather than discover that type of learner!

Learning styles theory does serve to provide useful reminders about the range of students in front of us and the range of activities that we could and should offer. However, students feel valued because we know them as individuals, not because we can define what kind of learner they are! We know that John prefers practical work to writing and Jane prefers group work to individual work; that Jamal prefers written texts to visual representations and Jessica prefers to listen to rather than read instructions – and scores of other things about them.

# Learning preferences

Our students do have **learning preferences** – these are complex and changeable. Should we attempt to differentiate by giving students activities that match their preferences, hopefully maximising engagement and success? Or should we provide all students regularly with all types of activity to develop them as rounded learners?

The best practice is to **vary learning activities** and to **allow choice** at times, such as whether students show their understanding via detailed writing, a presentation, a mindmap, even art or drama. Differentiation in this way maximises engagement through variety, ensures that students develop a full range of skills and motivates by allowing individuality.

# Individual interest

Altering timetable provision to cater for the interests of individual students is a can of worms that most schools are rightly cautious about opening. Where that interest reaches the level of an **exceptional talent**, a passion or a **vocation**, though, many schools are as flexible as they can be.

'I have always wanted to be a doctor and am going to apply to medical school in a year's time. I have been offered the chance to work-shadow a doctor on Tuesday mornings. Could I come into school an hour late on Tuesdays?'

'I have been selected to play for the county senior team. Could I miss PE on Thursday afternoons to go to train with the squad?'

Supporting individual students boosts their motivation. There are also many examples where this kind of differentiation can happen inside school.

# Supporting individual talents and passions

Most schools offer **individual music tuition**, through which thousands of students are able to flourish and enjoy improving their talents.

Yet there are very few schools where this kind of provision is available in other areas of the curriculum. How much more could we do to help the development of tomorrow's actors, sports stars, writers, business leaders, broadcasters,…?

There is an amazing array of less formal curriculum enhancement to support individual students' interests. This relies on staff goodwill or a bit of innovation:

- One school, instead of paying someone to look after its outdoor plants, pays them to teach a group of budding horticulturalists to do so
- In a number of schools, students advanced in ICT are involved in designing and maintaining the school website
- From archaeology to debating, from film-making to trampolining, many teachers run clubs for students who share their passion

# Structuring
# Learning

# Planning for differentiation

There are numerous ways in which we can plan and structure lessons to develop greater differentiation.

This chapter explains the key strategies in this area. It covers differentiation via:

- Curriculum
- Teacher expertise
- Outcome
- Task
- Resource
- Learning objectives
- Starters
- Plenaries
- Thinking skills

# Being creative with the curriculum

Government, exam boards and school leaders might decide the structure and content of curricula, but there is always space for **choice** and **creativity**! Many teachers review and alter provision to keep their practice fresh and relevant.

In one school, teachers are supported in changing exam board as often as they like. When they meet a new exam class, teachers assess their strengths and preferences, discuss the syllabuses with the students, then decide which will work best.

Keep updating schemes of work to reflect the technology and communication methods that your students are used to. Instead of more traditional options, could students:

- Create a blog giving an account of their progress through a project?
- Produce a webpage about volcanoes?
- Compile the pages of a social networking site to show their understanding of the characters from a novel?

# Developing choice within the curriculum

Differentiating for students by allowing them increasing choice gives them a sense of **ownership** and improves **engagement** and **motivation**.

With younger English students, Karen introduces several novels as a potential class reader. The students discuss them and then vote for the one they'd most like to read. Democracy reigns and the whole class study the novel with the most votes. As students mature, she offers several choices and students do much of the work in groups. The final stage is to allow students to bid individually or in groups for a novel they would like to read.

Dan follows a similar process with his Science students. Given a topic to investigate, he initially allows the whole class to make a democratic choice between four or five experiments to fulfil the investigation. As the students become more independent, more choices are allowed and several experiments run at the same time. Eventually, students devise their own experiments.

# Developing your match-making skills

All staff have particular expertise, at subject level or within their subject.

*How can they be brought closer together?*

All students have particular learning interests and learning needs.

Where classes tend to stay with the same teacher for all subjects, more flexibility about swapping classes can sometimes bring more focused learning for students – and can make teaching more enjoyable.

In secondary schools, some subject specialists make the most of their expertise within their subject by **swapping classes** for specific aspects of the course.

Take this a step further by **mixing classes** of students according to interest or need and putting them with the teacher whose expertise will be the best match to enhance their learning.

# Swapping and mixing

It is common practice for primary school teachers to swap classes so that each class has, for instance, music, art, technology or PE not with their class teacher but with a teacher in the school with greater expertise in one of these areas.

In secondary schools, where a teacher's degree focused on a particular historical period, or a particular aspect of biology, or a particular art form, or where they have a great interest in such an area, they might swap classes with a colleague whose expertise enables them to reciprocate in another area of the curriculum.

Mixing classes is common in PE, where students are often allowed to choose from a selection of sports, each delivered by a teacher who can push and support them further. In one English department, older students are allowed to choose from a selection of literature texts for their coursework and classes are mixed so that they are taught by the department's expert teacher on that text.

# Differentiation by outcome

Differentiation by outcome is undeservedly the black sheep of the differentiation family. It gets a bad press because it is open to being represented as a planned strategy when really no differentiation has been planned at all. It's by no means suited to all tasks and it's not a licence to ignore other forms of differentiation.

Students undertake the **same task** and produce a **variety of results**. How students respond to the task, and the level they reach, provide the differentiation. To use differentiation by outcome productively, you need to plan a task that is open enough to work on several levels. For instance:

- Create a piece of art with the title 'new beginning'
- Investigate how plants grow
- Put together a piece of drama to promote road safety
- Write about a character from a play or novel in your response journal
- Research and write a report on climate change and its impact

# Making differentiation by outcome work

Open tasks such as those on the previous page will produce a variety of outcomes, but students need guidance to ensure that you get the variety you were hoping for!

The task *'Research and write a report on climate change and its impact'* could bring anything from basic information paraphrased from one website; to a sophisticated explanation and evaluation of evidence, developing into a powerful discussion of our relationship with the planet.

To make differentiation by outcome as effective as it can be, the best practitioners:
- Set clear expectations of the kinds of outcome that would be appropriate
- Explain the time that should be spent on the task and how it might be used
- Show students examples of possible outcomes
- Ensure that students know the levels that they could reach and how to get there
- Challenge and support students to reach for the highest level they possibly can

One note of caution, however: take care not to be over prescriptive. Leave room for your students to explore, to be original and to surprise you.

# Setting different tasks

Where one task cannot be open enough to cater for the full range of potential performance in a class, differentiate by **adapting the task** or **providing different tasks**. This will enable all students to engage with a task at a suitable level of challenge and to achieve.

Generally speaking, avoid telling students which level of task to do. As much as possible, allow them to choose or to negotiate. Encourage **aspiration** and **effort** by emphasising students' potential to improve their ability through working on this task.

Try to design tasks so that students who are coping at one level can move up to the next one during the task. For example, once students have grasped single digit multiplication can they move on to two digits and then onto multiplying decimals; or once they have shown their understanding of a character can they find evidence to support their points and then analyse and explain how the author has influenced their views?

Remember that differentiation is fundamentally about the quality of our students' learning, not the quantity.

# The sum of the parts...

Individuals and groups can also be set different tasks that will feed into a greater whole. This invests a degree of responsibility with students, who know that the learning of the whole class will be dependent on them. It also means that each group or individual can study the one part they are assigned in far greater depth than if they were dealing with every part of the overall task. The work is shared out and all students benefit.

- Different groups each study one cause of an historical event. The groups then share their work with the class, beginning a debate as to which cause was most significant

- Groups each study one stage of an industrial process from raw material through manufacture to marketing. Put together, their work will provide a more detailed account than if every student had studied every stage

- Individuals each take responsibility for one page of a revision booklet for the whole class: tasks could include mind maps, sample answers, a glossary of key terms, etc

There's more about the role of groups and group work in the section beginning on page 81.

# Tasks to improve accessibility

What was the last piece of technology that you learnt to use? Did you:
- Follow the instruction manual step by step?
- Switch it on and experiment until you got it right?
- Sit with someone who knew what to do and ask them questions?
- Admit your inadequacy and get one of your children to teach you?

There are many routes to the same place. Tasks are usually a means to an end, not an end in themselves: we create them so that our students can develop skills and meet learning objectives. Differentiate tasks to allow students to learn the same thing in a way that suits them.

Offer choices in how they develop understanding by, eg:
- Reading
- Watching
- Listening
- Doing

Allow choices in how they express their understanding by, eg:
- Speech
- Writing
- Performance

# Homework tasks

Differentiated homework tasks incorporate **choice** and **independence**.
Students could:

Be allocated or choose from a selection of tasks to address an area of weakness

Be told that they will work in groups in the next lesson and that they are each responsible for preparing a separate part of what they will need

Choose an aspect of that day's or week's work that they would like to consolidate or research further and bring evidence of their work to the next lesson

Be given a set of increasingly complex tasks and invited to choose which level to attempt

Homework then becomes **an opportunity to extend the learning of individuals**.
Choice engages students more and ensures that work suits their interests or needs.

# Differentiated resources

Whether students are working on the same core task or a range of different tasks, refine provision further by **differentiating the resources** that they use.

More complex and numerous resources can challenge those with the highest level of learning potential; fewer and more accessible resources can ensure that everyone achieves.

- In English, students can be given different pieces of literature to analyse to develop their understanding of the techniques used by writers to create meaning

- In history, students can be given different sources to study to develop an increasingly profound understanding of the significance of a particular event

- In science, students can be given different sets of data to investigate to establish basic trends and then the reasons for certain anomalies

- In music, students can listen and respond to different pieces of music to discern more subtle dynamics and articulation

# Resource types

Differentiate not just by the number and depth of resources, but also by the type.

Teachers frequently use television programmes and DVDs and are increasingly exploiting the incredible number of clips on the internet. Always ensure that students are active viewers, considering questions as they watch. Differentiate further by giving different questions to particular individuals or groups.

For quantity and recency, the internet outstrips the books in any school library as the first choice for research. For reliability and relevance, though, the library often wins. Use both and compare their efficacy to enable your students to make discerning choices. Restrict students to websites that you have checked to ensure that time is not wasted – differentiate further by directing groups or individuals to different sites.

The best resources to engage students are often live ones: people – and animals if you are brave enough! Trips, theatre groups, speakers and demonstrations all provide a different and much more real insight that often sticks in the mind for years.

# Getting the starting point right

Any differentiation for the growth of a student's ability should be founded on a judgement of their potential to cope with new learning. Students with different starting points for a given task need different provision. Offer different levels of task or resource, or set different levels of objective or assessment for students of different potential. Encourage students to **challenge** themselves and allow them **choices** so that they can aim to reach higher levels.

It is vital to enable students to access the learning at a level that suits them as individuals. If they have to repeat what they have already learnt or cannot cope with a task because the previous stages are not in place, their progress will be limited.

The most innovative and flexible teachers are constantly forming judgements about whether students can start a task at a higher level. For instance, if the core learning for the class is the basic parts of a flower, do some students already know enough to jump to studying different types of flower?

# Maximising potential progress

With something as fundamental as ensuring that students access learning at the best point, **involve your students** in making these judgements.

As you embark upon a new topic, is there someone in the class who has just been reading a book about it and knows more than you would think? Might some students have insight into a particular area of the curriculum because of the job of a parent or grandparent or a place they have visited? Who attends a club outside school that has enabled them to develop a particular skill?

*Put letters A to E on the walls around the room when starting a new scheme of work. Ask students to stand by the letter that best represents them. To stand by A, students should be confident that with effort and support they will be able to do x, y and z. Reduce the level of knowledge or skill each time down to E, where students are reasonably confident that they will be able to do a, b and c. Where students stand can help you to determine groupings – you could create groups of students at a similar level or groups at different levels. You could, of course, make this less public by getting students to fill in a slip of paper.*

# Layering objectives

In the best classrooms, carefully differentiated learning objectives focus students on individually meaningful processes and outcomes and inspire them towards reaching their potential.

When differentiating for different levels of potential performance, **layer learning objectives** by selecting similar ones from different assessment levels or by creating a range relating to the potential spectrum of learning. If appropriate, use objectives from earlier or later years or curriculum stages.

Many outstanding teachers lead their students' learning by unpicking the often esoteric language of learning objectives rather than simply providing them.
Talk with your students about the differences between the layers. Encourage aspiration, tempered by realism, in challenging students to climb as high up the ladder as they can.

# Learning objectives and starting points

If students **access learning** at the **appropriate level** progress will be maximised. Several strategies will put the **student** at the heart of this process:

- Armed with the relevant assessment criteria and your feedback on their last piece of work, students are empowered to set their own objectives for the next steps in their learning
- Explain to the class the core objectives, then invite students to personalise them, adapting them to their own starting point, interests and needs
- Where work is spread over a sequence of lessons and students are at different stages, get students to set their own objectives at the start of each lesson. This encourages them to focus on learning rather than task completion. Better still, as a plenary, ask them to set their objectives for the next lesson, thus improving continuity from one lesson to the next

# Starters

To engage all students, starter activities need an element of differentiation. As students come in, have a **big**, **open question** on the board that the lesson will work towards, but that students can start thinking about and discussing straight away. Many teachers start with a couple of questions, or word games or short activities such as card sorting – whatever conveys the message: *'If you use your brain and work hard, you'll learn something today'*.

Alternatively, get students to respond to the objectives by discussing them with a partner or writing down some ideas. The level of their response provides differentiation:

- How do these objectives relate to recent lessons?
- What skills will you require to meet the objectives?
- How could we assess whether you have met them?
- At what level do you think that you can meet them?
- How are you going to challenge yourself today?

> *Occasionally, start by giving students the answer – they have to find the question! It could be almost anything, eg:*
> - *Seven*
> - *Oxygen*
> - *Metaphor*
> - *Green*
> *You will get some varied and original thinking in response!*

# How to phrase your learning objectives

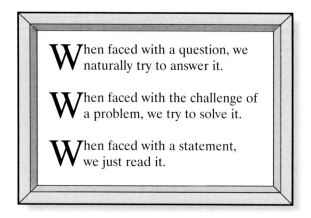

**W**hen faced with a question, we naturally try to answer it.

**W**hen faced with the challenge of a problem, we try to solve it.

**W**hen faced with a statement, we just read it.

**Engage students by making your objectives questions or problems, not statements.**

# What did you learn today?

Defying the students' urge to pack away and be first in the lunch queue, a simple plenary is squeezed in before the bell when you ask the question, '*What did you learn today?*' Different students will have learnt different things and you bring this out through who you invite to respond.

This kind of whole class plenary tends to involve only a few students. Asking students to **discuss the question in small groups** involves everyone. Ask a couple of students afterwards what someone else in their group learnt.

Don't always leave this or any other plenary question until the end of lessons. A quick review of learning at any point in the lesson can identify the need for further differentiation to support or challenge certain students.

# Meta-cognitive plenaries

Once students can articulate *what* they have learnt, challenge them to explain *how* they learnt it. What did they do to enable them to progress? As well as getting students to reflect, this reinforces the connection between effort and learning.

Don't let students drift into a routine response to a regular question. Try these:

*   How did today's learning relate to previous lessons?
*   How effectively did you learn today and why?
*   How are you going to use that learning?
*   How could you learn more effectively next time?
*   What was important about today's learning?
*   Where do you think that our learning will go next?
*   How does it fit into the big picture?

One level of differentiation in responses to these questions is provided by students' differing learning experiences during the lesson. Another level can come through directing particular questions at selected individuals or groups.

# The end of the beginning?

Very few lessons exist as discrete units – many of the questions on the last page emphasise the ongoing nature of learning rather than rounding off a task.

At key points during a scheme of work, ask students to write comments as a plenary, reflecting on their progress thus far. Also invite them to ask questions. Where patterns emerge this might inform your planning for the whole class for the remainder of the scheme of work. More likely, it will give you pointers to refine your differentiation for groups and individuals.

A simple but powerful way one teacher plans the endings of lessons:

Don't end a lesson with ■  End with !■  Or with ?■  Or with ■ ■ ■

Leave your students with something to think about, even if it is just where their learning will go next. However long their musings last, your differentiation is continuing beyond your lesson.

# Thinking skills – problems, problems, problems

Thinking skills are, of course, not limited to starters and plenaries. They form a vital set of differentiation strategies to use throughout lessons.

- Why is the bee population in decline and what should be done about it?
- How would you persuade a racist that their views are wrong?
- What, if anything, should we do to save polar bears from extinction?
- How could we make our school more accessible to disabled people?

Problem-solving activities involve **differentiated thinking skills** and have a range of possible outcomes. As they work through the problem, students will consider:

- What facts are known here?
- What opinions are there?
- Why is this a problem?
- How important is it?
- What ideas have we got to solve it?
- How well would they work?

The best teaching will integrate thinking skills into the curriculum rather than having thinking skills lessons as an adjunct. Problem solving is usually best done in groups, so that students can help to stretch each other's thinking.

# Inductive learning

In **inductive learning**, students are given a list or a set of cards with names or images of anything from animals to musical instruments; numbers to countries. They are asked to find groups with similar characteristics – often, individual items will belong to more than one group.

The process of classification helps students to understand the principles by which animals are organised into classes or musical instruments are put into families, etc. Older students can use this process to classify and analyse quotations from a play, data about a range of businesses, artistic techniques, etc.

**Differentiated thinking** is provided here by the difficulty of the classification process and the depth of analysis of the categories that students create.

# Bloom's taxonomy

With some thinking skills models, differentiation is partially integrated because the skills are hierarchical. Bloom's taxonomy is the best known of these. The depth and complexity of thinking required increases as we move up the scale.

| | |
|---|---|
| **Evaluation** | Judging and appraising; assessing and ranking |
| **Synthesis** | Blending and developing ideas; generating new ideas |
| **Analysis** | Classifying, investigating and examining ideas |
| **Application** | Applying and adapting ideas; manipulating data |
| **Comprehension** | Understanding and explaining; interpreting; defining |
| **Knowledge** | Identifying facts; remembering; listing; finding |

The top-ranked skills are often viewed as the province of higher performers and many teachers differentiate via tasks that require increasingly demanding cognitive skills. This is perfectly sound as long as all students have the chance to move up the hierarchy.

But stay flexible: the skills are not always hierarchical, depending on the topic and the individual. Some students will, at times, find it easier to evaluate ideas than to apply them.

Why
Differentiate?

 Ability, Potential
and Difference

 Structuring
Learning

 Refining
Learning

 Groups and
Grouping

 Challenge
and Support

 Assessment and
Feedback

 And
Finally

# Refining
# Learning

# Ready, steady, go!

As well as differentiating in the way we structure our lessons, there are other differentiation strategies we can use *within* lessons. This chapter covers several of these, including pace, choice, negotiation, questioning techniques, modelling and language. We'll begin with the pace of learning.

Differentiate by pace by setting students a task to complete as quickly as possible. The speed and agility of thought required reinforce knowledge and skills and are good practice for exams. Use with a wide range of tasks, including:
- A set of mental arithmetic questions
- Scanning a text to find key pieces of information
- Recalling the names of the planets in the right order

Also use fast pace:
- To liven up question and answer sessions (especially when recalling facts)
- To improve students' focus during group work, eg 'You've got 3 minutes to…' The sense of urgency can be really motivating and exciting
- To give students a sense of the pressure often found in the work environment
- To force students to make decisions to create a quality, concise response

# Ready, steady, slow!

It is equally important to **slow things down** at times to encourage students to think.

- Give students 'think time' before they begin a task: how will they go about reaching the highest level they can?

- Allow students time to reflect when they get assessed work back, when they review their own work and when they set themselves targets. As a starter, give five words, numbers, images, elements, dates, etc. Ask students to think of several answers to *'Which is the odd one out and why?'* Obvious answers will come in seconds but, given time, more subtle 'odd ones out' will emerge

- Don't allow students to start a piece of writing or creative work until they have spent at least ten minutes producing a plan

- Structure learning around open questions or problems. Give students time to think about these questions or problems – and to find their way to the answers

# Planning choice

While planning individualised learning for 30 different students is impossible, planning choice so that students can personalise their own learning, and so that all individuals are accommodated, is realistic and is one of the most effective differentiation strategies. Choice can work in many ways:

- **Sequence** – set several tasks and let the students decide in what order to complete them
- **Task** – give students a choice of written assignments, experiments, exercises, calculations, art forms, etc, each of which can deliver the same learning goal
- **Approach** – set a task, from showing how writers create atmosphere to explaining basic algebra, from researching an historical event to making a model. Before starting, students choose how to approach the task. What resources will they use? Will they opt to work alone or together? How will they organise their time? What will their end product be like?
- **Ways to present work** – in what different ways can students present work for assessment? Eg using ICT, oral presentations, drama or film
- **Level** – when differentiating for ability, enable students to choose to tackle more challenging levels than they are used to

# Why choice?

Choice is significant because it puts students at the centre of their own learning. Allowing them choice creates **ownership** and **engagement**, which lead to **motivation** and **success**. The relationship of trust and respect between teacher and students is also enhanced.

When you offer choice, success depends on setting clear parameters. For instance, be explicit about the purpose of the task, the learning objectives, the level students should be learning at and how their learning will be assessed. You'll then feel confident that your students are empowered to select the best option for their learning, not the easiest one or the one their friends are choosing!

Differentiate not just the type of choice, but the degree of choice for different classes and individuals – some will cope better than others. Gradually increase choice over time as you get accustomed to letting go of the wheel and your students become accustomed to taking it.

# Invite negotiation without losing control

Negotiated differentiation is particularly suited to more confident, independent students.

Outline a forthcoming task – this works best with sizeable ones. Make clear the learning objectives and assessment criteria: the parts that are not open to negotiation. Allow students time (or set them a homework) to put together a proposal for a **personalised version** of the task, justifying how this will enhance what they produce.

Some will prefer to stick with your structure; others will successfully negotiate with you which parts of their proposal they will be allowed to keep. From planning to final product, these students will engage in some very original thinking and learning.

# Fostering negotiation

Almost any task spanning a number of lessons will enable you to allow an element of negotiation.

In ICT, your focus might be to teach students how to use spreadsheets. There would be core objectives, such as layout, basic formulae and conditional formatting. Your standard task is for students to put together the accounts of a fictional small business. Students might negotiate personalised versions using a real business run by someone they know, using data relating to one of their interests such as performance data of their favourite football team, or using data from another one of their subjects. They might extend the task to investigate ways to make the business more profitable or to merge the spreadsheet with a database. They might elect to put together a report evaluating the efficacy of spreadsheets or a presentation to demonstrate how to use them.

With any of these negotiated versions, students will fulfil the core objectives and often achieve much more. They will be motivated by a greater sense of ownership and interest.

# Closed and open questions

Like choice, when used skilfully, questioning is a key differentiation strategy that engages students, caters for individuals and enhances learning. Effective questioning is a talent – and like all talents it can be developed and improved. Involving all students, keeping their attention, dealing with the unexpected and knowing where to pitch questions all add up to a formidable challenge.

**Closed questions** – with short, definite answers – are useful to check understanding and establish key information. Limit their use, though, since they do little to develop learning or get students thinking.

**Open questions** – based on personal ideas and opinions and without a single 'right' answer – will invite students to think and to get involved in the learning. Open questions can often be accessed at different levels, especially when followed up with extension questions. (See next page).

You can also differentiate by choosing who will answer. Make sure that students know that you might pick them, then target your differentiation precisely: *'Sadie made a point earlier about X. Now that we also know about Y, how does that change things, Tariq?'*

# Follow-up questions

Whilst open questions get your students thinking, the way you follow them up determines the depth of their thought.

Teachers who use questioning effectively respond to students' answers with further questions, exploring ideas and opinions and helping students to extend their insight. They encourage discussion as a fundamental part of a lesson – quality discussion provides quality learning and engages students at all ability levels.

After a student answers a question, try one of these:

- *What evidence can you provide here?*
- *How did you reach that conclusion?*
- *What would be the effect of that on …?*
- *How could we prove this right or wrong?*
- *Does anyone have any questions here?*
- *Could we look at this in another way?*

- *What does that imply about …?*
- *Does everyone agree with that?*
- *Yes, but what if …?*
- *How significant is that for …?*
- *Can you explain … a little more?*
- *Can anyone add to that point?*

# How long can you wait?

You won't always want to target individuals; it is sometimes appropriate to throw a question open to the whole class, but we've all experienced the following:

> *You ask a question. A hand shoots up and you gratefully invite that student to answer. If no hand goes up, after a couple of seconds of tortuous silence you give in and provide the answer, or maybe make the question easier.*

In this way, many discussions are dominated by more confident, quick-thinking students and most of the class know that they don't need to think or get involved.

Providing **longer wait time** after asking a question encourages all students to think and is more likely to elicit an answer:
- Ask a question and give ten seconds of think time before taking responses
- Ask students to discuss the question with the person next to them, and then be ready with a response. Checking and developing their ideas with a partner first, makes students more confident in front of the class
- You can target differentiation further here by asking different pairs to consider the question from different points of view

# Dynamic discussion

After a student has answered a question, the instinct for most teachers is to praise the answer and move on, or repeat or rephrase the answer and move on.

This is where a second type of wait time comes in. As your students get used to follow-up questions, sometimes just wait after a question has been answered. Often, this is where your best thinkers and students with the greatest potential will take the baton and run with it.

- They might challenge or build on ideas
- They might ask new questions or put everything in perspective
- They might be logical or creative; empathetic or critical
- They might not go exactly where you envisaged, but so much the better – they are developing their own and everyone else's thinking!

Young children's natural curiosity drives them to ask hundreds of questions. Fight to maintain this in your students: **curiosity is a great motivator**.

# Modelling

One of the key ways we learn is by imitating others; one of the key ways we teach is by demonstration. Modelling, like follow-up questions, is an aspect of the teacher's art that cannot be fully planned in advance if it is to be effective. Modelling is an extremely powerful strategy because rather than showing a final product, it shows the **processes** involved in getting there.

The most useful modelling is when you create something 'live' in front of your students, revealing as you work the thinking, modification and shaping involved in producing an excellent piece of work. Be prepared to think on your feet and to respond to questions as they arise. Don't be tempted to show the class something you prepared earlier – this shows *your* skill, but does little to develop *theirs*!

Throughout your teaching, model the **attitude** you want your students to adopt. Show that there's nothing wrong with making mistakes – unless we fail to learn from them. Be prepared to try new things, to take risks, and openly endeavour to improve your teaching. Talk about how you got to where you are: through effort and motivation and by challenging yourself to improve.

# Using modelling to support differentiation

Modelling suits a tremendous variety of skills, from solving simultaneous equations to writing to create atmosphere; from drawing people's faces to passing a ball; from formatting text on a computer to compiling a mindmap to aid exam revision.

When modelling, cater for the range of possible outcomes by showing the characteristics of different types of work and of work at different levels. Explain the differences between one level and the next. Don't let students sit passively as you do the work – ask questions and encourage them to comment on and ask about what you are doing.

*Having gathered the class at the front of the room, Dan models a particular skill, explaining up to five levels at which students could achieve. At various points, he invites students who think they are ready to hold up two numbers: the level they are confident they can reach, and the level they are going to challenge themselves to work towards. If he is happy that they are challenging themselves enough, he gives a thumbs-up sign and they quietly go off to start work. He continues to model the task to the remaining students until everyone has started.*

# Dialogue and language

Language is the ultimate tool of the teacher's trade. You use it in a myriad of ways to inspire, support, challenge, cajole, manage and lead your students.

By instinct you vary your language use for different classes, groups or individuals. Reflect occasionally on how you **differentiate your communication**: it is the hardest part of your work to monitor or plan, but has a huge impact on learning.

- Are your explanations clear to all?
- Are you using the right level of technical subject language for different students?
- How well does your dialogue with individuals support and challenge them?
- If asked a question, do you give the answer or help students find it themselves?

Consider how many times you get it right. Even better, consider how many times you get it right without needing a script and without time to think, surrounded by a classroom full of students. How many other jobs expect that sort of skill?

**Why Differentiate?**

 **Ability, Potential and Difference**

 **Structuring Learning**

 **Refining Learning**

 **Groups and Grouping** ◀

 **Challenge and Support**

 **Assessment and Feedback**

 **And Finally**

# Groups and Grouping

# Setting

How we group students at class level and within classes has a significant impact on their learning and is another key area of differentiation. Any 'setting' based on assessment of performance is a bit like the latest technology – as soon as it exists it is out of date. Just as the next steps in technology are already being conceived and created, students have already moved on to another piece of learning in which some will make significant progress and perform better than ever before.

Given that we now know the vital role of effort and motivation in improving ability, it is difficult to justify saying that a school differentiates provision through setting. Unless there's a system that allows flexibility of movement across sets there's a glass ceiling over the students.

If your school or department chooses to differentiate in this way, base decisions on visible indicators, such as interest, commitment and effort, etc. Take past performance into account only as a guide to (not a predictor of) future potential. Above all, ensure that movement between sets is possible for students who work hard, achieve well and make good progress – and for those who don't.

# Differentiation through 'ability' grouping

Whereas the ability of each student is highly complex, sensitive and changeable, the setting of classes and ability groupings within classes is often simplistic, insensitive and rigid. It's an awkward marriage.

In the most innovative schools, ability grouping is based on a student's motivation, the potential growth of their ability and their responsiveness to supported challenge. It makes far more sense to group together students whose potential development *will* be similar than whose past performance *was* similar.

Telling students that they are in a certain set or group 'for now' puts emphasis on effort and the future. Those in the 'top' groups know that they will need to work hard to stay there. Those in other groups know that they could move up by working hard: they have something to aspire to.

In any ability grouping structure, sets still contain a mix of 'ability' and potential and thus the learning still needs to be differentiated for students' ability to grow. There are also, of course, many other reasons to differentiate.

# Choosing groups

Whilst teachers usually have limited control over which students are in their class, how they group those students at different times for different purposes gives them immense opportunity.

The best group size for most purposes is three or four, maybe five: big enough for a variety of ideas; small enough for everyone to get involved. Bigger groups can result in some members not getting an opportunity to join in, or sitting back while others do the work.

Some teachers find it easier to fix certain groups within their class for a half term: one group might be based on a particular learning need, another on a mix of preferred ways to learn. Get students to write their groups down, or you could display them on the wall. As students enter the room, tell them to get into their colour groups, or shape groups, or whatever suits the age and subject.

# Who chooses, and why?

Most teachers allow students to choose their own groups, or where teachers do choose they often do so at random. Yet, getting the composition of groups right is a key differentiation strategy that can produce engaging and highly productive learning for every one of the unique learners in your classroom. The type of groups you use and which students you put in them need careful planning to deliver results.

Groups might be chosen on the basis of:

- Putting students with similar potential together to work on a task – or mixing them up with other students
- Students' social or communication skills
- Friendship groups – either keeping friends together or apart
- Similarity or diversity of opinion or a host of other ways, many of which are explored in the pages that follow

# Some groups and when to use them

- **Friendship groups** help students to share openly and support each other. They are good for sensitive or personal subjects. The downside is that they are prone to consensus and so might not stretch students' thinking. If allowed to, students tend to choose to work in friendship groups, and not always for the learning benefits!

- **Groups of students with similar learning potential** suit tasks differentiated for ability. Students of similar potential need opportunities to work together, so that they can challenge and support their mutual progress

- **Groups of students with mixed learning potential** suit tasks with a variety of outcomes where all can make a valid contribution that shows their skills, from project work to group presentations. Some will emerge as leaders; some will learn from their peers; some will be stretched by supporting others

- **Single gender groups** work well in certain situations, eg if you are studying gender issues and want to spark lively debate! They're also useful in classes where one gender outnumbers the other or tends to dominate discussion

# More groups and when to use them

- **Learning need groups** are highly effective. After assessing a piece of work, group students together who have displayed the same weakness and give them a series of tasks that address that weakness to work through together

- **Groups of students with similar learning preferences** motivate students and facilitate high quality outcomes. Putting students together who like role-play, or mind mapping, or problem solving or discussion can enable them to hone their skills. Be aware that such groups can occasionally suffer through clashing egos!

- **Groups of students with varied learning preferences** will develop students' social skills. Students will have to compromise, support each other and perhaps work on improving their less favoured areas. Equally, each individual has the chance to shine, to help others and to learn from others

- **Groups based on choice** of task or topic motivate by enabling students to pursue their interests. Choosing a sport to play, a book to read, a country to study or a model to build, often makes these groups highly focused. You need to be able to manage the unpredictability of how many will choose each option

# Differentiating through group roles

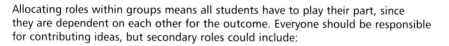

Allocating roles within groups means all students have to play their part, since they are dependent on each other for the outcome. Everyone should be responsible for contributing ideas, but secondary roles could include:

* **Group leader** – facilitates progress
* **Note-taker** – records ideas
* **Time keeper** – monitors task completion
* **Summariser** – checks agreement
* **Spokesperson** – provides feedback
* **Resource finder** – whatever the group needs, they grab it

Different students will have different strengths. Allow groups to choose their own roles at times, but also differentiate by ensuring that everyone experiences each role over time.

# Rainbow groups

With careful planning, rainbow groups will deliver sustained and productive group work where all students are engaged in differentiated learning. They work best with groups of the same size.

In their initial groups students work together to complete a task, each group undertaking a different but linked task. You then reconfigure the groups so that each new group contains one student from each of the original groups (organise this yourself, eg by giving everyone in the initial groups a letter from A to E and getting the As together, etc.) Each student shares their knowledge with their new group which then goes on to use that combined knowledge to tackle a new level of task.

Your students could work in rainbow groups to:

- Study types of graph, then evaluate which to use in which context

- Analyse how characters are portrayed, then decide the most effective ways to create their own characters

- Explore different software, then judge its efficacy for a range of applications

# Envoys

Once students have completed a set of different tasks in groups, to avoid long feedback sessions use envoys. Each group sends out an envoy to another group, to whom the envoy explains their work.

In one version, the envoy then answers any questions and returns to their original group. Use envoys in this way to get each group to compare the qualities of two works of art or two essays before widening out into a class discussion of five or six examples.

Alternatively, the envoys continue on their mission until they have visited *all* of the other groups, spending a minute or two with each. Use envoys in this way to try to get students to persuade each other which film is best, which type of exercise is most beneficial, which technique works most effectively, etc.

The role of the envoy is differentiated, but other students can take on, eg: preparing the envoy for their mission or questioning visiting envoys and compiling comparative notes. Sometimes envoys work better in pairs.

# Triads

Working in threes with specific roles, students can produce highly focused work.
If all three study different texts or data beforehand, as B questions A about what they
have studied, C writes notes. The roles rotate twice so that all three have shared their
knowledge, listened to others and contributed to a comprehensive set of notes. All
three are then ready to move on to the next stage.

Alternatively, C can act as an observer who could
consider, say, the skills being demonstrated as A
interviews B for a job then provide both with feedback.

Triads are also useful for peer assessment.
Whereas pairs of students reviewing one
another's work can soon run out of ideas,
studying the strengths of a piece of work
and areas for improvement in a triad can
result in more productive dialogue.
Differentiate carefully the combinations of
students in triads and the level of task they
take on. If they are not going to rotate roles,
these too can be differentiated.

# De Bono's Hats

Edward de Bono developed the concept of **six approaches to thinking**, each denoted by a coloured hat. Working in groups of six, each student 'wears' one of the hats and contributes ideas **from that perspective** to the group:

White – facts and information
Yellow – positive ideas, benefits
Green – creative, innovative ideas

Red – emotions and responses
Black – negative ideas, problems, barriers
Blue – meta-thinking, monitoring the process

Differentiate either by allowing students to wear their favoured hat to engender the best possible ideas, or by trying other hats to develop broader skills. Topics can be anything from analysing the issue of abortion to reviewing the impact of technology. Differentiate further by giving each group a different topic.

An alternative approach is to get small groups to generate ideas on a subject from each perspective by all wearing the same hat for a few minutes, then changing to the next one, etc. This can avoid some students drawing a blank and involves everyone in each skill.

# Guided learning

Guided groups have been commonly used for reading and increasingly for writing, particularly in primary schools, but they can be used for almost any task at any level.

The guiding principle is for the teacher to sit with a group of between four and six students and give them more intensive support and challenge as they progress through a task. Group together students with similar learning potential or with a similar learning need that the task is addressing.

The remainder of the class will need to be working independently, but this is an ideal opportunity to differentiate by allowing them the chance to take responsibility. Learning Support Assistants can be invaluable in helping to monitor the rest of the class.

# Guided learning at work

A group of students might have come to light who all have a weakness in their use of simple sentences, or who are all struggling with long division. As the teacher sits with this group to give them guided support, the rest of the class might be independently working on extending the skills that they have in these areas, completing exercises that can be self- or peer-assessed that challenge them to use compound sentences or to divide using larger or decimal numbers.

Alternatively, while the rest of the class works on an extended piece of writing or on individual projects, the teacher takes a group out who have similar levels of potential to provide additional guidance that will stretch and support them to maximise their achievement.

This is just one way in which you can differentiate by providing targeted challenge and support – the next chapter explores some others.

Why
differentiate?

 Ability, Potential
and Difference

 Structuring
Learning

 Refining
Learning

 Groups and
Grouping

 Challenge
and Support

 Assessment and
Feedback

 And
Finally

# Challenge and Support

# Support and challenge for all

All students benefit from support: it enables them to face greater challenges successfully. Of course, the type and amount of support you provide will be different for different students. Support can take many forms, eg:

- Everyday **one-to-one classroom exchanges** between teacher and student
- **Intensive help** from learning support with, eg literacy or numeracy
- **Mentoring** – schools that use mentoring report huge benefits
- **Course booklets** and task sheets
- The **interdependency** of students working in pairs or groups
- Students **emailing experts** in a particular area of study
- A **question** to help **scaffold** a student's thinking
- A **resource** or **website** to look at
- The chance to **discuss their work** with someone working at a higher level

Over time, as they tackle challenges successfully, students become more resilient and develop strategies to deal with similar challenges independently. They can then benefit from support to face even tougher challenges.

# Overcoming obstacles

The individual programmes put together for many students with special educational needs provide highly differentiated support. Some schools have broadened this practice to provide individual programmes for 'gifted and talented' students; a few use it for all students.

In class, at times, support will address the particular learning needs that inhibit a student's progress; at other times, it will be appropriate to circumvent these to enable the student to progress in subject skills. Strong liaison between teacher and support assistant about how to make the learning accessible is key to effective differentiation. Try to adapt tasks so that students with SEN can face the same challenges as others in developing their thinking skills and meeting learning objectives, rather than finding that the only challenge they face is the obstacle in front of them every day.

# Supporting students with SEN

Gavin caters for students with weak literacy skills by sometimes allowing them the option to show their understanding orally rather than in writing. Gizela caters for students who experience difficulties in presenting information by sometimes allowing them to use ICT rather than drawing graphs to record data.

Laura adapts resources for visually and aurally impaired students to ensure that they can access the curriculum in the least obtrusive way possible. With both impairments, she ensures that they sit in the most appropriate place when they move around the classroom, for instance to do group work.

Rajiv is aware that the changes in routine that can be stimulating for most students can be unsettling for those with Asperger syndrome and need to be explained in advance. He adapts language to make sure that it is clear and direct, avoiding humour, jargon and euphemisms. Whilst trying to improve the social skills of children with Asperger's, he is aware that at times it is appropriate to allow them to opt out of group activities.

# Students supporting each other

Students working ahead of most of the class can often provide support for their peers. When the teacher is busy, it can be hugely beneficial for students to have this kind of support readily available. If combined with a system of learning buddies, it is very discreet, suiting students who are reluctant to ask for help.

This is equally useful for those providing support – the most effective way to embed learning is to teach it to others. This process reinforces learning, puts it into the student's own language and connects it to other learning. The penny drops that bit further when we articulate something rather than simply absorbing it: learning becomes more active, less passive.

Students supporting their peers are also enabled to reflect at higher levels on the significance of what they have learnt and how it fits into the bigger picture. When your highest achievers are **supporting their peers** in this way, **support their thinking** by giving them a couple of challenging questions to ponder and try to answer afterwards.

# Learning buddies

Sit students together in pairs or threes as **learning buddies**. When they are stuck, or need someone to check their work, or at other designated times, students can consult their buddy. Buddies should be students who can work together and learn from each other – best friends are often too close for this. Buddies tend to be students working at similar levels, but all sorts of combinations can work.

Once it is explained to them by one of their peers, children will often grasp something that they were struggling with when an adult explained it. As learning buddies get to know each other, they tend to develop an instinct for using language that their buddy will understand.

Peer support works best when it is used regularly and becomes part of the culture of the classroom. It then becomes a natural part of the learning process. If it is only an occasional event or the teacher has to coerce and cajole, it will be less effective. It can take a while to create this culture, but persist – it is worth it.

# Extending learning

Differentiation by extension is, in essence, additional work for those who complete a task, although the danger is that those who get to the extension work are the least thorough rather than the most successful – they are often boys. Check that the 'fast finishers' have achieved the learning objectives.

The best extension work invites students to consider high level questions, to undertake research and develop their thinking, to produce creative and exciting work, to work together or independently on challenging and enjoyable tasks. It is stimulating and motivating in just the same way that the core learning is, students receive meaningful feedback on their work and the work is seen as the logical next step in their learning.

# Quality, not quantity

Extension work should do exactly what it says – extend the students' learning.
A useful mnemonic is:

**HOTS**, not **MOTS**: Higher Order Thinking Skills, not More Of The Same.

**MOTS**
*Do another 50 sums!*
*Write another story!*
*Go around the obstacle course again!*
*Do another self-portrait!*

**HOTS**
*What patterns can you see here?*
*How significant do you think this is?*
*How could you use this in daily life?*
*Why might some people not like this?*

There's no incentive to do MOTS – repeating what you've just done is dull and a waste
of time. It can seem like a punishment for being too clever and the student learns not
to finish as quickly next time. The challenge of HOTS, however, is something to relish –
a clear development of learning and, therefore, worthwhile.

Quality not quantity; **HOTS**, not **MOTS**.

# Differentiation by extension

When students have achieved the objectives for the core learning, move their thinking to the next level:

- Add the next layer of complexity compared to the original task
- Set them the task of evaluating their work and the techniques they have used, or comparing their work to a more sophisticated product
- Invite them to consider how the work they have just done relates to the current topic and connects to prior learning
- Send them off to research in greater depth one particular aspect of what they have just learnt
- Ask them to look at their learning from a different perspective
- Challenge them to analyse the significance or relevance of what they have learnt

If you find yourself providing extension work on a regular basis for certain students, consider whether the core learning is challenging enough for them.

# Extra-curricular enrichment

Just as extension differentiates by encouraging greater depth, enrichment differentiates by providing greater breadth. Historically, enrichment activities have been seen as the preserve of those designated gifted and talented. In the best schools stimulating enrichment opportunities are offered to all students.

Enrichment days, master classes, trips and summer schools provide an array of fantastic experiences that make learning enjoyable, foster better relationships between students and staff and support the creativity that so often gets squeezed out of the curriculum. It's not hard to see the benefits for everyone.

One primary school enrichment day involves the whole school in staging a festival. Students spend the first part of the morning in a carousel, working with musicians, dancers, costume makers and caterers from outside the school. They then choose one area to specialise in for the remainder of the morning. In the afternoon, they hold the festival in front of an audience of parents. Everyone gets involved, new talents are found, leaders emerge and all students experience a range of learning and experience success.

# Master classes and trips

Master classes give students insight into higher levels of learning that can inspire them for weeks afterwards. Many secondary schools run such classes for primary school students; many universities run them for secondary school students. Subjects as diverse as building robots, forensic science, film-making and composing music, provide fantastic opportunities for students to find interests beyond the school curriculum. Often, classes are held at weekends and attended by only a small number of students – it is so much more effective when they are held in school time and everyone selects from a range of options.

Trips to the theatre, art galleries and museums, field trips and residential visits enrich students' education in so many ways. They bring new experiences to many, stretch students' thinking and develop their personal skills. They enthuse, engage and motivate and make learning much more real.

Monitor the range of students who get involved in activities outside school time. Are some not taking part because they lack the money for trips, because they can't get home from after-school clubs, or because they feel they won't fit in?

# An enriched curriculum

Given the positive benefits of enrichment, the best place for it is within the curriculum. Set aside a lesson once in a while to:

- Do that experiment that your students will love and will learn from, even though it's not an essential part of the curriculum

- Give your students some team-building, problem-solving tasks to refresh their thinking for the weeks ahead and to introduce issues you'll be studying together

- Get a guest speaker to extend students' learning in an area where they have shown particular interest

- Take your students out to experience things in the real world, rather than just in text books, from the cycle of the seasons to the geography and history of the local area

- Show your students what makes you passionate about your subject specialism, be it Mozart or building rockets; tragedy or DNA

The experience of teachers who do this is that the time spent on enrichment is repaid many times over in **improved motivation and engagement**.

# Using display to support learning

Another way to support learning is through display. Make classroom display powerful and organic by focusing it on current work. Devote space to supporting and challenging learning, perhaps including:

- Notes, plans and mind maps put together in class
- Lists of key words in this particular topic, differentiated
- Structures and guidance to help students to negotiate their way through tasks
- Images and artefacts
- Students' questions and other students' responses displayed on Post-it® notes
- Questions posed by the teacher to promote thinking skills
- Assessment criteria for the current work
- A list of sources of further information

Some students will use the display as their first port of call when they need support, others will find it useful when you, their teacher, are busy. As well as building independence in students, it frees up time for you to focus on higher impact support. Differentiation is developed through the range of material on display and how students use it.

# How far can your students leap?

Each individual's ability to cope with challenge is different. It varies from one subject to another and between aspects of a subject. When it comes to judging how much challenge a student can cope with, there is no substitute for knowing your students and knowing their learning potential:

- How confident are they and how much risk will they be prepared to take?
- Do they have the right skills in place to face this level of challenge?
- What level of challenge will motivate them most?
- How far could they be stretched and what support will they need to get there?

Ideally, let your students have at least an element of choice here to encourage ownership and effort. Students tend to be more ambitious when involved in setting their own level of challenge: it gives them greater permission to struggle or fail. There is a fine balance to strike with students' confidence: they should be confident that they *can* succeed and improve their ability (if they put in the effort), not that they *will* succeed (irrespective of the effort they put in).

Why
Differentiate?

 Ability, Potential
and Difference

 Structuring
Learning

 Refining
Learning

 Groups and
Grouping

 Challenge
and Support

 Assessment and
Feedback ◀

 And
Finally

# Assessment and Feedback

# Assessment mode

Having looked at how we structure learning, how we refine classroom delivery, how we group students and how we provide challenge and support, the last key area where we can differentiate is through assessment and feedback.

Boys tend to perform better in multiple choice tests; girls tend to perform better in coursework. Many students express their understanding better orally than on paper. Some students will convey their ideas more effectively by creating a web-page rather than writing a report. Some will prefer to express themselves in original ways through performance rather than in more traditional modes, for example recording a news show rather than writing a newspaper article.

When planning assessments, try to strike a balance between, on the one hand, covering a full range of assessments that will help to prepare students for the future and, on the other, enabling them to follow their preferences and show their skills and understanding in the best light. Cover all relevant assessment modes over time, but also differentiate regularly by allowing choice of assessment mode so that students can work in ways that will motivate them and thus maximise their learning.

# Assessment criteria

It is accepted good practice to ensure that students are aware of the criteria against which they are being assessed. Use self-assessment and peer assessment regularly so your students are used to **applying the criteria**, not just reading them.

Equally important in enabling students to achieve is that the criteria are **flexible** and **broad** enough to assess every student in a meaningful way. In the very best practice, teachers set assessment criteria at a range of levels to cover the **potential performance** of all students in the class. This might mean accessing criteria from previous and subsequent curriculum stages: where necessary use these to free your students to learn at the level that suits them.

Set criteria – or help your students to choose criteria – that will enable them to succeed and progress, but that will involve them having to struggle to get there.

# Using assessment mode to differentiate

**Formatively**, assessment is most purposeful when it ascertains learning and progress and identifies the next steps that a student should take. Only through a varied range of assessment modes can students, teachers and parents gain a detailed picture here and work to develop a wide spectrum of skills.

With final, **summative** assessments, be as flexible as you are allowed to be to enable students to succeed:

- In some subjects, creative, original responses will meet the criteria just as effectively as traditional essays or reports

- Investigate in what different ways, from podcasts to poems, students can express their ideas

- Where students have a particular aptitude, eg for ICT, film, art or for public speaking, make it possible for them to use this to their advantage

# Effective feedback

One of the places where the relationship between student and teacher is most focused on the **learning of the individual** is in the feedback (oral or written) you give each student about their work. Effective 'assessment for learning' will mean that there is more focus on comments than marks and grades. Comments will indicate how well the work has met the assessment criteria and identify the next steps.

In the very best practice, feedback will value the effort and motivation in a piece of work and will emphasise that student's progress. Clear personalised targets will aid further progress towards the individual student fulfilling their potential. The student might be asked to write a comment in response to the teacher's comment, or the teacher will find time for a very brief discussion with individual students.

The differentiation here is comprehensive – feedback is about the individual student's learning and progress.

# Making feedback work better

It is ironic, given the individual differentiation provided by effective assessment for learning, that its timing is so often unhelpful. Providing comments and targets on completed work means that the feedback comes too late to inform the student's learning on that piece of work. The next time the student is doing a similar piece of work – one where the targets will be relevant – could be weeks or months away, by which time they are likely to have been forgotten.

It is much more powerful to make an assessment **halfway** through and set targets for the **remainder** of the task. Students can then act immediately to develop themselves in line with their targets and teachers can provide extra support or challenge to ensure that students achieve as well as possible.

Thus, differentiated assessment becomes an integral part of the present and future learning process, not simply a measure of past performance.

Don't feed back, feed forward

# Differentiated targets

Make sure that *all* students, from the highest achievers to those making slower progress, are set targets that incorporate:

**T** ime — When will progress towards targets be checked?

**A** chievability — To build confidence, emphasise success and renew motivation

**R** elevance — So that they are focused and meaningful for that student

**G** rowth — Building skills and abilities, not about marks or behaviour

**E** ffort — That will make the difference between the student stalling or progressing

**T** eacher — Providing the necessary support

**S** tretch — To ensure that the student makes real steps in their learning

Involve students in negotiating or setting their own targets. This makes them more personal, creates greater engagement and is more likely to lead to success.

# Self-assessment and independence

Use self-assessment to give students some **responsibility** for differentiating their own learning. Provide a bank of resources – perhaps in a shared area of the school's computer network – that will support improvement from one level to the next in each assessment focus. When students have assessed their own work, set them a task (perhaps as homework) to use the bank of resources to target their weak areas. The resource bank could include guidance and a range of exercises on anything from capital letters or algebra to developing databases.

These tasks discourage excessive teacher dependence and develop students' independent learning. The best practitioners provide video clips of a teacher demonstrating and explaining a skill and an electronic exercise where each step is marked as right or wrong as soon as the student has typed in their answer. Students get instant feedback on their progress and take increasing control of their own learning.

# Self-assessment to inform planning

Occasionally, give students a full list of the assessment focuses for a subject or for a particular aspect of the subject. Ask students to 'traffic light' each statement:

**Green**
I am confident
in this area

**Amber**
I need to work
on this area

**Red**
I need help
here

This exercise will give you and your students the basis for planning work differentiated to their needs.

It can also help you to differentiate the brief but vital one-to-one chats that you have with students, where those who underestimate their skills might need their confidence boosting and those who overestimate their skills might need a reality check.

# Inviting feedback

To check that the balance is right for your students, ask them to provide feedback when they have completed an assessment. A simple continuum can be completed in seconds, where at one end the assessment criteria were too easy to meet, and at the other end too challenging.

As a plenary, occasionally invite students to ask questions about the current work, about their progress or about any aspect of their learning where they feel unsure. Use their responses to refine your differentiation in the coming lessons.

To encourage students to **reflect** more on their progress, set a homework with just two questions:

*1. What could you do to improve your learning?*
*2. What could I do that would help you to improve your learning?*

Most students are highly appreciative of teachers who invite feedback on their teaching and will offer helpful ideas to enhance your differentiation for them.

# Ipsative assessment

Develop in your students the use of **ipsative assessment**, ie measuring their **current performance** not against grades, averages or their peers, but against their own **prior performance**. How much progress have they made in their learning during the lesson, during the last week or during the last half-term?

You may be surprised at how your students, particularly those who play computer games, are used to assessing themselves in this way outside school. The determination to beat one's best score is a great motivator.

This kind of assessment is automatically differentiated for each student. The emphasis on progress boosts confidence and encourages sustained effort. The teacher's role is to provide the learning opportunities and support that students need to secure the next steps in their progress.

Take it a step further by asking them to consider their **potential performance** – how they can make further progress in the next lesson, week or half-term? How much do they think they could improve? Their responses can be eye-opening.

# Success and failure

You and your students will not always get the level of challenge right, but try to avoid erring on the side of caution. Faced with too little challenge students become complacent and fail to make progress. Pushing them too far occasionally will remind them of the importance of hard work in overcoming problems and will help them to get used to coping with failure.

Keeping the right balance between success and failure for each student is extremely difficult, but this is the art of great differentiated teaching and learning.

In the right balance, success outweighs failure but both have a part to play:

**Success**

Confidence, engagement, enjoyment, valuing learning

**Failure**

Identifying targets, resilience, knowing you are being challenged enough

Motivation, renewed effort

Why
Differentiate?

 Ability, Potential
and Difference

 Structuring
Learning

 Refining
Learning

 Groups and
Grouping

 Challenge
and Support

 Assessment and
Feedback

 And
Finally

# And Finally

# Developing differentiation

Developing differentiated learning has meant an evolution in the role of the teacher from a simple imparter of knowledge to a multi-skilled professional who **leads** and **guides** groups and individuals towards their peak.

*Start small and climb at a pace that suits you and your students:*

Choose a few new strategies – a next step for you and your students

As you practise and refine these, they start to become habit

Once these are becoming embedded, look at the next stage

We tend to create comfort zones around ourselves – it is particularly understandable that teachers do this, since we want our students to feel secure. Many aspects of differentiation require us to challenge our comfort zones and to move away from the security and safety of whole class routines; but creating new working practices for individuals and groups can make students feel more comfortable when they find they are more engaged and can make better progress.

# Labels

Whilst out shopping, you see a jar that takes your fancy. You are not sure what you will put in it or where it will go, but you buy it nevertheless. Back at home, you decide to put your biscuits in it. You have some similar but not identical jars already, so after a few days you stick a label on it saying 'Biscuits', so that you and others can easily identify it. It moves from being a jar that currently contains biscuits to being your biscuit jar.

After some time, you decide that although it has functioned perfectly well as a biscuit jar, you want to use it for something else. You try to peel the label off, but only manage to rip off the top part, leaving a sticky mess behind. You scrape most of it off with your nails, leaving just a few gluey remnants. You put it through the dishwasher, but they are still there. You attack it with an eraser and remove some more, scrub it with a scrubbing brush and a bit more yields, try every chemical cleaner in the cupboard and wear it down further. But there's still a stubborn, greyish residue that you cannot remove. You wish that you had never labelled it in the first place.

> **Labels are designed to stick. Avoid labelling your students, whether by ability, attitude, target grade, learning style or anything else.**

# Individuals

*In an age where everyone involved in education is trying to cater more for the individual, it is both ironic and understandable that labels abound.*

30 individuals in a class can seem like a daunting prospect, so in some ways it seems natural to follow our basic human instinct to classify things.

- Each individual student comes to us with different abilities and preferences
- Each individual has different needs in terms of support and challenge
- The abilities of almost every student will improve steadily over time, but there will be vast differences in how fast they grow and how much progress each individual will make

However, differentiation is not about creating an individual programme for every student. It is about continually **improving our provision** for groups and individuals and **opening up learning pathways** so that students have opportunities to flourish and fulfil their unique potential. When we get this right, we help our students to achieve a state of 'flow', where optimal learning brings greater motivation and creates a **cycle of growth**.

# Climbing mountains

The most significant factors in ensuring that each individual develops their abilities and achieves their potential are:

- The effort they put in
- The degree to which we as teachers can provide differentiated learning that stretches and supports them
- The belief of all parties, including parents and the school as a whole, in the concept of growth

Teachers do awesome things in their quest to help *all* their students achieve. The measure of success is not a student standing on top of a mountain, but rather their successful journey to the summit. It is this that will enable them to go on to climb more difficult mountains and, ultimately, to climb by themselves.

Our students will all climb different mountains and will do so in different ways. The future tense is key: the question for us must not be which mountains did they climb yesterday, but which ones could they climb tomorrow, and how can we help them reach the summit?

# Further reading

***Boys, Girls & Learning Pocketbook***
by Ian Smith. Published by Teachers' Pocketbooks, 2010

***Effective Classroom Communication Pocketbook***
by Richard Churches. Published by Teachers' Pocketbooks, 2010

***Finding Flow***
by Mihaly Csikszentmihalyi. Published by Basic Books, 1997

***Growth Mindset Pocketbook***
by Barry Hymer. Published by Teachers' Pocketbooks, 2014

***Mind in Society***
by Lev Vygotsky. Published by Harvard University Press, 1978

***Mindset: The New Psychology of Success***
by Carol Dweck. Published by Random House, 2006

***Six Thinking Hats***
by Edward de Bono. Published by Penguin Books, 2000

***Taxonomy of Educational Objectives: The Classification of Educational Goals***
by Benjamin Bloom. Published by Longmans Green, 1956

# About the author

**Peter Anstee**

Peter has taught in comprehensive schools in Essex for over 15 years. Having led a highly successful English Faculty for seven years, he has since held various whole-school responsibilities, including: improving the achievement of the more able, assessment and leading the development of teaching and learning.

He has run training courses on Fast-tracking and on ICT in English. He has led whole-school INSET sessions in every school he has worked in, on subjects such as underachievement in Year 8, independent learning, student motivation and differentiation. He has written for the TES and provided consultancy services to schools and local authorities.